THE
CALL

A Radical Redemption

TYWANNA CHRISP

authorHOUSE®

AuthorHouse™
1663 Liberty Drive
Bloomington, IN 47403
www.authorhouse.com
Phone: 1 (800) 839-8640

Published by AuthorHouse 01/25/2017

ISBN: 978-1-5246-5679-9 (sc)
ISBN: 978-1-5246-5677-5 (hc)
ISBN: 978-1-5246-5678-2 (e)

Library of Congress Control Number: 2016921128

Print information available on the last page.

KJV
Scripture quotations marked KJV are from the Holy Bible, King James Version (Authorized Version). First published in 1611. Quoted from the KJV Classic Reference Bible, Copyright © 1983 by The Zondervan Corporation.

NIV
Scripture quotations marked NIV are taken from the Holy Bible, New International Version®. NIV®. Copyright © 1973, 1978, 1984 by International Bible Society. Used by permission of Zondervan. All rights reserved. [Biblica]

Acknowledgements

I first give all the honor and love to my ABBA JEHOVAH, His SON JESUS CHRIST and to the HOLY SPIRIT.

I most sincerely and lovingly thank my husband, Albert Chrisp for his technical support.

Thank you, Gale Watson and Carolyn Alexander for your encouragement in forwarding this book.

Thank you, Pastor I. Cherry, for your love and spiritual support throughout the years.

I thank you, Bishop W. Thomas Sr., Rev. Johnson, Bishop Saunders, Apostle G. James, and Rev. H. Greene for being living examples of dedication to the will of GOD.

Thank you Cynthia and Mary for being my spiritual sisters and my friends.

Contents

Chapter One

"The Call is JEHOVAH"

"I will stand upon my watch, and set me upon the

tower, and will watch to see what He will say unto

me and what I shall answer when I am reproved.

And the LORD answered me, and said, Write the vision,

and make it plain upon tables, that

he may run that readeth it."

(Habakkuk 2:1,2)

NORMAL:

I was living like many people in America, enjoying the life of free choice and opportunities. Here I was, in my fifties, black, female, married (2nd time), had a family, a good job, and a home. Although I had come from a plebian environment; the oldest of eight kids, I considered myself fortunate. I was feeling lively, healthy, and hopeful. I went to church most of the time and was on the usher board. I was "nice" to others and I had a few friends. Now, I also had my own life's share of making *foolish decisions* and I bore the repercussions of them... just like most people. **So, I felt <u>normal</u>.**

Then, one winter's night in **1997**, I happened to turn on the TV in my bedroom and became transfixed on a **documentary**

about wars, slavery, the holocaust, and oppression... starting from Biblical times up to the present. It made me break down in uncontrollable tears because I suddenly realized that **mankind had failed GOD!** We are *still* full of greed with no compassion for others; we ignore the Ten Commandments... even the <u>Bible</u>; we are self-centered and evil-minded. I felt the fear and horror of man's old sin nature and I prayed to GOD to *please* forgive us humans and have mercy on us! (Wow! ...Now *where* did this sudden burst of emotions come from?)

*After this experience, I began to feel the need to know more about the Bible...more about GOD...more about JESUS. When I expressed this to a church member, she advised me to join a **Discipleship** class that had just begun. (...But, I thought a Discipleship class was for "seasoned" members or leadership?) She assured me that my desire to "dig deeper" was all I needed. **So I joined the Discipleship class.**

DREAM:
Soon after that revelation (a month later?), I had a **<u>dream</u>** about **<u>owls</u>**. This dream was unlike any other dream I ever

had. It was like watching a movie screen with <u>me</u> as the main character. Now, at the bottom **left** side of this "screen" I saw myself walking upward on a sandy colored dirt road that led straight to the <u>top</u>...to the sky! As I was walking up the road, I looked over to my **right** side and saw houses, grass, and trees. There were ***human-sized brown owls*** moping along on the ground, in the trees, and also on the <u>roof</u> of one particular house that was closest to me. Now, one owl was more noticeable because it sat boldly in a tree that was "closer" to my road. It appeared to be dominant over the other owls.

(...still walking...)

After observing the *scenery* on my right, I proceeded to walk along the road. Suddenly, I looked **up**...at the very top (in the sky), and saw a **giant white owl** with ***wings expanding across the whole "frame" of the dream***, from the farthest left to the farthest right of the "dream". Every white feather glistened like glass, each with such a beautiful, *pure* light illuminating from them! The white owl's face was massive, yet peaceful. HE appeared to be slowly descending towards the brown owls. (The brown owls seemed to anticipate the coming of the white owl.) Then I looked back over at the brown owls and I shrugged my shoulders as if to decide that they had nothing (else) to do with me, so I turned around and began to walk back towards where I had come from. (End of Dream)

DREAM TOLD/INTERPRETED:

This **"owl"** dream was so profound and disturbing that I had begun sharing it. At work, I decided to recall the dream to my friends and coworkers. They first explained to me that the Pope had been visiting nearby and that many people seemed to be having dreams or visions during this same time. While that information afforded me no real explanation of my dream, it gave me a sense of comfort knowing I wasn't alone and that just maybe there is a reason or purpose for this dream.

Later, I told my dream to my discipleship teacher who told me to go home and pray and ask GOD to reveal the meaning of the dream to me. She said that she will pray and ask GOD also, so that when we meet again next week for class, we would discuss what we had received from Him.

That week, I prayed and prayed for an answer, but seemed to get no response. However, my discipleship teacher explained to me that **owls** represent <u>wisdom</u>; the brown owls represented "bad" wisdom, while the white owl was "good" wisdom. She then said that she feels the dream is preparing me for a "test". She said that I should fast and pray and read my Bible. (This I began to do.)

(I later discovered that the white owl was <u>GOD</u>! ...Amen!)

THE "TEST":

One night, weeks after the dream, I was praying on my knees in my upstairs hallway for my family. (My church/ discipleship class had requested that we pray for our families.) While praying, I *felt* something come over me and I thought, **"This must be the HOLY SPIRIT!"** So, I was elated and I exclaimed, "Thank You, HOLY SPIRIT!"

Before this, I had always watched other people "act in the spirit" in church and I would think to GOD, "GOD I don't know if they are pretending or not, but I dare not even think about playing with You. If being 'in the spirit' happens to me, then I *will <u>know</u> for myself that it is real. Otherwise, I do <u>not</u> intend to fake it."*

Well, after that prayer for my family...after feeling the "Spirit", I kept feeling "different" yet receptive of the new feeling. I felt I was now "walking in the spirit" like I've been hearing of. I would gradually feel this "spirit" in me <u>learn</u> (relearn) everything in my home: my rooms, my <u>touch</u> of items, my <u>view</u> of every room.... *(**Wow! I'm walking in the spirit**!)* <u>EXCEPT</u>! I <u>also</u> began to feel uncontrollable sexual responses as though some invisible person was violating me at its will (from within?). I knew that lately, my marital sex life was not so active at this point, but would GOD allow the HOLY SPIRIT to "satisfy" me in such a way? I thought to myself, "Now I *heard* that GOD will satisfy all our needs, but something about this was just <u>not</u> <u>right</u>. I had to <u>tell</u> somebody! I needed an explanation...fast!

*(Now, the deeper explanation of what took place in me must be reserved for grounded theologians; that there be no confusion as to what is of GOD and what is not.) All I can say is that this was the beginning of my "**test**"!*

At my church, I met with my discipleship teacher and I told her about my surreal encounter. She responded, "That's <u>not</u> the HOLY SPIRIT". I said, "Oh no! I *knew* something wasn't right!" She then prayed over me and anointed me with oil and I felt something lift off me that gave me a *lighter* burden. But, that was not <u>all</u> that I needed, as I quickly discovered. As soon as I got in my car to leave the church, I could "feel" the spirit "learning" my steering wheel as I held it! "Oh, no!" (**I <u>prayed</u>**.)

Well, now that I *knew* that it was <u>not</u> the HOLY SPIRIT, but the "other" spirit, and I began to **cry out** to GOD, both outwardly and inwardly! "Why GOD?"...When You know I love You and take You seriously? Why, when I love You so much? What have I done? Please forgive me! What must I do now? Oh, GOD!!! Help me!"

Going through...

And So began the saga of my crying... and praying and fasting... and praying and reading the Bible ... and praying... and crying ...and praying. (For about a month or two?)

"Trust in the LORD with all thine heart;
and lean not unto thine own understanding..."
(Proverbs 3:5)

CHURCH REJECTION:

Well, during this "test" period, I had also decided to tell my Pastor and Youth Pastor about it; But I guess they didn't know how to receive (understand) such a story. I began to feel *contaminated* in the <u>worst</u> way. I began to feel that maybe I *should* stay away from the church...and I <u>did</u> for a short while. Then, I remembered the **<u>owl</u> <u>dream</u>** (hope) that GOD had given me...and I <u>held</u> <u>on</u> to that dream and that <u>hope</u> for dear life! So, I chose to go back to church and I trusted that **GOD gave me that dream for a purpose.**

Why art thou cast down, O my soul? and why art
thou disquieted in me? hope thou in GOD: for I shall
yet praise Him for the help of His countenance.
(Psalm 42:5)

Now, also during this time, I began to warn my family members that, *"It's <u>true</u>!... there really <u>is</u> a spiritual world of evil...and of <u>good</u>! ... And I am a living witness!"* I tried to warn them to turn to <u>GOD</u> and to pray for their families. Well, that went over like brick in water; They simply thought I had had a nervous breakdown; that I had most certainly <u>lost</u> it. I was told, *"Maybe you have a brain tumor."* (Like my <u>sister</u> who had recently passed away!) I was asked to get a CAT Scan. I said that although I knew that was not my problem, I would get a CAT SCAN to prove that it was not a mental or physical condition, but <u>spiritual</u>. (Of course, my scan was <u>clear</u>.)

But I say unto you, Love your enemies, bless them that curse you, do good to them that hate you, and pray for them that despitefully use you, and persecute you...
(Matthew 6: 44)

Now, during this **test period**, I had also decided to <u>remove</u> my "contaminated self" from my household. Yes, I left my family! I certainly was not going to let an evil source "learn" any more of my home or my family! So, I was now staying over another relative's place ... *until*...until what?

I realize that I had left my "house family" and went to "another" family member's dwelling ...but, it's still <u>family</u>!

Why? I guess because I knew that these relatives would at least pray for me and would have others pray for me.

Anyway, you can guess that when they took me in that I had my share of concerns for them as well. Quickly, however, I found myself referring to the Bible scriptures for everything. I realized that there was nothing happening in my life that hadn't already been addressed in GOD's Word. Reading the Bible day and night would give me a feeling of peace and assurance that GOD knows all about my fears and of my true love for Him; that He was with me throughout this "test" and that He would never leave me. After all, it was He who gave me the dream to prepare me...for "whatever" He has for me. **GOD's Word** had become my lifeline and my only real trust...my only true hope.

Thy Word is a lamp unto my feet and a light unto my path.
(Psalm 119:105)
So then faith cometh by hearing, and hearing by the Word of GOD. (Romans 10:17)

One revelation that I did learn was that whenever I would say aloud, "JEHOVAH" or "JESUS CHRIST", that my body would <u>tremble</u>! So, evil entities <u>tremble</u> at the holy and mighty names of our LORD!

*Now, I was still Baptist, being the oldest of eight children, and therefore having more time to be "watered" with the Word in Sunday School. One sister who *was* Baptist like myself was raised by our aunt in yet another Baptist church; That sister is now deceased.

> ***Fear thou not; for I am with thee: be not dismayed;***
> ***for I am thy GOD; I will strengthen thee;***
> ***yea, I will uphold thee with the right***
> ***hand of MY righteousness.***
> ***(Isaiah 41:10)***

*Shortly (a week?), I went back home, **trusting GOD** to see me through. So, here, I would cry out to the LORD <u>daily</u>; fasting, praying, washing my face before the LORD, and still wondering ***why me***, when I loved Him and believed in Him so truly? Also, at night before I slept, I would place a Bible at the top of my head and another opened Bible on top of my blanket, across my hips to keep the enemy away from my mind and away from my "reproductive" area.

One *late* night, as I was fasting, I fell on my face before the LORD on my kitchen floor. I asked GOD to **take my life** "now" if I could be with <u>Him</u> rather than let the enemy have any part of me. (Nothing happened.) Then, just after I got up from the floor and was about to give up hope, I hear a soft, kind voice in my head that said, "Wait on the LORD...." I felt such a relief and <u>peace</u>; and I knew that *this* was from GOD! So, when I went to bed that night, I was able to **sleep peacefully.** (I had not slept in peace since all this "testing" began.)

> ***Wait on the LORD*** *and be of good courage,*
> *and He shall strengthen thine heart.*
> *(Psalm 27:1)*

> ***Peace I leave with you, My peace I give***
> ***unto you: not as the world giveth,***
> ***give I unto you. Let not your heart be***
> ***troubled, neither let it be afraid.***
> ***(John 14:27)***

After that, as I "digested" GOD's Word every day and let the HOLY SPIRIT teach me, I began to feel the love of GOD slowly and daily release me of each "burden" that I was carrying. I began to feel the peace and love over me every day and night as I prayed, read the Bible, and fasted. This love was so pure, so right, and I could actually feel the arms of JESUS' love, holding me, comforting me....

...A ram in the bush...

During this time, GOD had paired me with a Christian coworker and friend who seemed to know my heart and said that she believed GOD was doing something special in me. It was refreshing to know that someone actually understood and had compassion towards me. So, when she told me that her church was having a **retreat** scheduled just weeks away, I immediately agreed.

As soon as we arrived at the retreat and located our rooms, we walked over to the campus church. We were then told to get on our knees and pray outwardly and openly to GOD. As I closed my eyes and prayed and cried out to my LORD, I could hear myself began to talk louder and I stood up with my arms stretched up to Him. Suddenly, I was crying out to GOD in a *different* language! I knew what I was praying in my heart, but it came out in **a different tongue**! Then, as I opened my eyes, I noticed that almost *everyone* was standing like me, with outreached arms, speaking in different tongues...all over the church! It was <u>GLORIOUS</u>!

> *And I will put My Spirit within you,*
> *and cause you to walk in My statues, and ye*
> *shall keep my judgments, and do them.*
> *(Ezekiel 36:27)*

> *If the Son therefore shall make you*
> *free, ye shall be free indeed.*
> *(John 8:36)*

After that retreat, it seemed that every time I would pray, I would almost immediately start speaking in tongues. This was so amazing that I would just ask GOD to please make sure it was "HIM" and not a trick from the enemy. Also, I began to want to know what my LORD was telling me, so one day, as I was praying to GOD in my bathroom, I asked Him to please let me understand what He is saying so I can <u>do</u> it! Within minutes, the tongues switched to **clear language**. I heard my LORD! (And I *still* hear Him <u>today</u>.) "Pride, change it...hold the baby...Pray in the LORD...Stay in the LORD...."

And I will pray the Father, and He shall give you another Comforter, that He may abide with you forever; Even the SPIRIT of TRUTH; whom the world cannot receive, because it seeth Him not, neither knoweth Him: for He dwelleth with you, and shall be in you.
(John 14:16,17)

<u>**GOD changed my life!**</u> Very soon, He sent me out to evangelize: I was led to use fliers of salvation and love: "***The Roman Road***", "***GOD Loves You Right Where You Are, But He Loves You Too Much To Let You Stay There!***" (I had heard this message/story on the radio.) Also, GOD had me to place 7 potatoes per plastic grocery bag to hand out *wherever* <u>He</u> would send me. I would pray over the potatoes after I bagged them and I would ask GOD where He wanted me to go. Then, I would give out the potatoes along with the flyers of salvation and hope. I went out into the streets and door-to-door. Wherever GOD would tell me to go, I went! The blessings I experienced where amazing!

Go ye therefore and teach all nations, baptizing them in the name of the Father, and of the Son, and of the Holy Ghost. Teaching them to observe all things whatsoever I have commanded you: and, lo I am with You alway, even unto the end of the world. Amen.
Matthew 28:19,20

For the preaching of the cross is to them that perish foolishness; but unto us which are saved it is the power of GOD.
1 Corinthians 1:18

For we are labourers together with GOD: ye are GOD's husbandry, ye are GOD's building.
1 Corinthians 3:9

At one time, I recall that my discipleship teacher had told us to each pray and ask GOD what it was He wanted us to do? Well, as I prayed to GOD in my basement, He clearly told me that I would "speak" for Him. What?? I thought, "LORD, are You sure you want "me" to speak? Now, LORD You know that I've never been a good speaker...that I get very nervous and start stuttering and stammering and losing train of thought as I speak...*me*?

My "ABBA-Daddy" (HE taught me to call Him that.) has used me in so many ways. He made me understand the <u>Trinity</u>. (Only GOD knew that I still had some reservations about the Trinity.) During my prayer times, the HOLY SPIRIT had begun telling me "JESUS is GOD" every time I would pray... until one morning, it suddenly became crystal clear to me! JESUS is "GOD the <u>SON</u>"! ...So, <u>yes</u> HE *is* GOD! ...The TRINITY!...(GOD the FATHER, GOD the <u>SON</u>, and GOD the HOLY SPIRIT.) Amen!

> ***For thou art my hope, O LORD GOD:***
> ***thou art my trust from my youth.***
> ***(Psalm 71:5)***

My precious FATHER gave me many dreams and visions. He also made me speak for Him... to encourage some and to warn others in need of redirection/repentance.

Some of my friends have been witnessing my walk and have drawn closer to our LORD.

No weapon that is formed against thee shall
prosper; and every tongue that shall rise against
thee in judgment thou shalt condemn. This is
the heritage of the servants of the LORD,
and their righteousness is of Me, saith the LORD.
(Isaiah 54:17)

I am crucified with CHRIST: nevertheless I live; yet not
I, but CHRIST liveth in me; and the life which I now
live in the flesh I live by the faith of the Son of GOD,
Who loved me, and gave Himself for me.
(Galatians 2:20)

TEACHING AND TALKING:

JEHOVAH taught me to <u>love</u> Him...to truly fall in love with JESUS, and to be so grateful to the HOLY SPIRIT. (What a triune, **complete love**!) He gave me that "walk-on-water" faith. He did something wonderful to my heart. I pray that I never lose the love, the zeal, or the "life-line" dependency upon Him.

Greater is He that is in me than he that is in the world.
(1 John 4:4)

HE *still* talks to me: "Train in the LORD...trust in the LORD...cleanse your heart...I chose you...Be holy...clarify My Name...walk everywhere...be strong...We love you...I love you...trust JESUS...Beloved...Serious One...behold Him... many days...I take care of you...No one takes away...Tell them My Name...My Name is JEHOVAH...Tell them My stories...."

*I am in awe as I reflect on how I was a grateful <u>usher</u> when it all began. Over time, <u>GOD</u> spoke to others to make me a deacon...then <u>later</u> a Youth Pastor/Elder. <u>HE</u> gave me gifts to teach, to preach, to evangelize, to heal, and more! <u>HE</u> really gave me a Five-fold ministry. Praise GOD!

I can do all things through CHRIST
which strengthens me.
Phillipians 4:13

GOD is in control! He programmed and predetermined my purpose! He <u>snatched</u> me out of the darkness (death) **into the <u>light</u>** (life)!

GOD is <u>Real</u>! JESUS CHRIST is <u>LORD</u>!

Bless the LORD, O my soul: and all that is within me,

bless His Holy Name!

(Psalm 103:1)

The Deceiver...

P.S. - The enemy *will* <u>try</u> to come back and attack you, especially where he has attacked you before. After my "test", he had "tried" to create doubt around me to make me think I was not really delivered or chosen by GOD.

During my "contaminated" period, I had tried to do warfare <u>myself</u>. I had decided that I would "get rid of that enemy" (fight) with the warfare information I had gleaned during a Bible Study at church. I went into praying, reading scripture, and "denouncing" the enemy upstairs in that hallway. During the "battle", I found myself with my <u>back</u> and <u>legs</u> up against the wall, with my head and shoulders still on the floor. That's when I called out to my nephew to bring me the phone and I called my spiritual friend and coworker who went into prayer and warfare agreement with me on the phone; The battle <u>stopped</u> and I was able to bring my legs back down.

To this day, I still don't recall "how" I suddenly got into that position with my back and legs up against that wall.

> *GOD is our refuge and strength, a very present help in trouble. Therefore, will not we fear, though the earth be removed, and though the mountains be carried into the midst of the sea; Though the waters thereof roar and be troubled; Though the mountains shake with the swelling thereof.* Selah **(psalm 46: 1-3)**

While some will tell you that you can deliver yourself, it is important to know that true deliverance comes from the LORD! **HE** <u>will</u> fight your battles! You need to <u>know</u> "Who" to call! You need to <u>know</u> "Who" has the power! You need to <u>know</u> our CREATOR, our GOD JEHOVAH, and our LORD JESUS CHRIST. Call His <u>NAME</u>! **"JESUS!"**

...One night, not long after my deliverance and being <u>strengthened</u> in the WORD, that evil spirit had tried to "revisit" me sexually while I was sleeping. Well, I went into spiritual <u>warfare</u>, calling on **JESUS**, and standing firm in the LORD, Bible in my hand and said, "Oh no you won't!" - I began to read scriptures, walking the floor, and praying to JESUS out loud. Then, when I suddenly realized that my actions alone could not send that enemy away; that I knew <u>nothing</u> really...that's when I cried out loud to JESUS, "**JESUS, <u>You</u> please fix it! I don't know how...but, <u>You</u> know! Please do it!**" Suddenly, I felt like I was in another dimension! Then, this "electro-magnetic sound" around me made a "SNAP!" sound, then another "SNAP" sound towards my window! (Something went out my window!) Suddenly, the **peace** was around me and I <u>knew</u> that **my JESUS did it!** Amen.

"Thank You, JESUS!"

And the LORD said, "If you have faith as a grain of mustard seed, ye may say unto this sycamine tree, Be thou plucked up by the root, and be thou planted in the sea; and it shall obey you.
(Luke 17:6)

"Be still, and know that I Am GOD: I will be exalted among the heathen, I will be exalted in the earth."
(Psalm 46:10)

I have come to understand how we are "chosen" by GOD long before we are known to our mothers in the womb. GOD already knows the plans He has for us; He knows where we are going and when He will step in and change our lives to draw us to Himself. Well, GOD chose to "change" me at <u>His</u> right timing for me and cause me to know Him and to have a personal relationship with Him! I see now how **GOD holds the master plan** for our lives; He has always been with me, even years ago when I was sent to Sunday School/church as a child; <u>**He was there**</u> (JEHOVAH SHAMMAH) when I lost my first tooth... when I fell and scratched my knee... when I told my first lie...when I went to school...when I had my son...when I first married...when my husband fought me and I later divorced him...when I was in the world... when I remarried...when I laughed and when I cried...when I couldn't understand why...when He prepared <u>me</u> and my husband to be the ones to take my dying sister's kids into our home and raise them in the LORD ... when He <u>snatched</u> me out of the darkness into His marvelous light! ...when I was lost (thinking I knew everything and that I had control of my own life/destiny), but *now* I <u>see</u> (with the spiritual eye... through <u>His</u> eyes)... HE has been with me all along! He never left me! He knows me...yet, He still loves me! What an AWESOME GOD!

"...one thing I know; whereas I was blind, now I see."
John 9:25

"Yet I will rejoice in the LORD; I will joy in the GOD of my salvation. The LORD GOD is my strength, and He will make my feet like hind's feet, and He will make me to walk upon mine high places..."
(Habakkuk 3:18, 19)

One thing I have learned in this journey is that GOD is so in <u>control</u> of our lives:

1. GOD planned the timing of my marriage and then prepared my husband's and my hearts to receive my dying sister into our home along with her two children whom we finished raising.

2. GOD had prepared me to fast before going to California and bringing my sister back with us. My other sister and I had been studying under an <u>herbalist</u> during that time ... cleansing us! A fast!

3. After taking on the children, GOD blessed us with the house (#7) to raise them in. The "dream" and the "test" took place in that very house. I got <u>salvation</u>; "HOLY GHOST" FIRE while living in that house. Later, GOD allowed me prayer vigils at our home and to have sweet peace to permeate in that house. (Children would feel so peacefully happy and <u>at</u> <u>home</u> in our house.)

4. GOD gave me dreams that came to pass and ministries, like children's ministry and street evangelism, etc.

5. My ABBA-DADDY prepared my heart, and prepared my spirit (dreams) to ground me in Him for the journey ahead.

* I encountered the right people along all the right paths in my journey to bring me to where I am today. So, when I think of the "timing" of it all and how everything keeps falling into perfect place for GOD's purpose for me, I carry the assurance of His love and protection with me; After all, He's my ABBA-DADDY!

And I'm His child. So, I'm a child of the KING of KINGS! I am royalty!

JEHOVAH is the one and only ALMIGHTY GOD, CREATOR of heaven and earth! He makes the winds and the waves obey His will. He created us (mankind) in His own image. He is our <u>FATHER</u> and He <u>loves</u> us so much that even when we turned away from Him and chose to do things our own way and did what was evil in GOD's eye, He reached out to save us! He sent His only begotten Son, JESUS CHRIST to earth to show us the way back to Himself and to take on our sins at the cross. JESUS bled and died, fought with the devil, and <u>won</u> victory over death...for <u>us</u>! Yes, GOD loves us so much that "GOD the Son" came to die for us on the cross. What love! No greater love than this! To <u>know</u> Him is to <u>love</u> Him!

...How can I (you) *not* love Him <u>back</u>?!!!

JESUS keeps calling...He keeps knocking at the doors of our hearts...Just <u>answer</u> the door when He knocks! Answer **"The Call"**. ...Say, "<u>Yes</u>!"

> *Therefore if any man be in CHRIST,*
> *he is a new creature:*
> *old things are passed away; behold,*
> *all things are become new.*
> **2 Corinthians 5:17**

> *And we know that all things work together*
> *for good to them that love GOD,*
> *to them who are called according to His purpose.*
> **(Romans 8:28)**

Anyone who has had a supernatural encounter and personal **love** relationship with GOD will not have to be convinced of HIM and HIS WORD. HE *is* **GOD the FATHER, GOD the SON, and GOD the HOLY SPIRIT!**

> **"He that is of GOD heareth GOD's words; ye therefore**
> **hear them not, because ye are not of GOD."**
> **(John 8:47)**

I do pray that my "radical redemption" experience will give someone a deeper faith in our Creator and will wrought belief where there may have been doubt. (*LORD, I believe. Help thou mine unbelief! Matthew 9:24*)

> **Rejoice in the LORD, O ye righteous: for praise is comely for the upright. Praise the LORD with harp: sing unto Him with the psaltery and an instrument of ten strings.**
> **(Psalm 33:1,2)**

P.S. - I invite you to share in the journal section regarding excerpts from dreams, visions, and Words from GOD which have directed my life over the years and continues to guide me, even today. Many encounters will not be shared because some are personal in nature, especially where others are involved. GOD has also given me my own *personal* warnings and encouragements...and hope.

Do you have the gift of interpretation? Has GOD revealed the meaning of dreams to you? Can you understand the following dreams? Try and see...

Chapter Two

DREAMS

On August 14, **2014**, while on vacation with my husband, I woke up from a most disturbing **dream** (of urgency!). I had a dream... of **babies**...of the <u>world</u> (globe) in the sky: One "dark" baby was on the floor of some domain, needing (wanting) tending to...it's bottom legs were gone. The baby was on its back on the floor...and I didn't care to help it(?). Then, abruptly, I was <u>outside</u> and I was talking to a person, when I suddenly saw, up in the open blue sky, our <u>earth</u>, so <u>vividly</u>, like through a high powered lens or telescope! The waters were <u>very</u> blue; the land was an even deeper blue. Super-vision!

Now, as I was talking to the person, whose back was to the sky and who was unaware of the globe, I became **alarmed** at the sight and <u>yelled</u> to the person to "turn around and <u>see</u> what I see!" (Then, was the earth turned *upside down*?)

Then, quickly, *another* vision appeared showing a large <u>chunk of earth</u> and a white baby being *forced* into the crack/opening in that chunk of earth! (The baby looked like one of those old-fashioned life-sized dolls with the plastic head, arms and legs.)

Then, I see the <u>same</u> chunk of the earth, but with the **baby "upside down"**, being forced into the same crack/split in the earth-chunk. Wha-a-at???

I am <u>very</u> disturbed and alarmed in the vision!
...Help us! ...end times? ...Emergency!! Alarm!! Humanity!

(Oh, yeah. There was "something" about the earth's <u>crust</u> around it.)

Later that day, as my husband and I headed back home from Myrtle Beach, SC, I became aware of the blue "sky" as we drove along the highway. I think,

"What does all this mean, LORD?...What must I <u>do</u>?"

As we pull into "South of the Border" along the way, and my husband answered his cell phone, I look out from the car and notice a family (Spanish/Indian?) taking pictures of their little girl seated on the cement figurines by our parked cars. As they finished and began to walk towards the stores, that's when I noticed the little girl holding the <u>same</u> <u>type</u> of doll as in my dream!! ...Wow!! *(I hadn't seen <u>that</u> <u>doll</u> since I was a girl!)*

"LORD! Help me know what You are saying!"

Oh yes! I remember that at the end of the dream, I was in the air, on some invisible object/board/platform and I was about to head *towards* the globe/world, but first, I <u>looked</u> <u>back</u> towards the (people?) and said to them, "**OK, <u>get</u> <u>ready</u>** ... as I motioned to them to <u>follow</u> <u>me</u> ... to the globe ... (to <u>do</u> something!) ...What??

*It was as if I was anticipating the **right timing** for us to **"head out" to this problem.**

DREAM

December 24, 2015

This morning I woke up around 2:30 AM. After a moment, I realized that I had dreamed another dream relating to the **"End Times"**. Once again I was left with a concerned feeling for mankind to be watchful and "get ready".

This dream was a short dream whereas I was looking outside of my dwelling into a yard/field full of **green** and healthy **trees and shrubbery**. (It was daylight.) A **supernatural pressure** or force came upon the midst of the land and "pressed" all of the trees and shubbery <u>downward</u> and outward towards the ground. (Was it in the wind? A <u>controlled</u> wind pressure? Was it the Hand of GOD?) *I ponder on this.*

Well, as soon as I saw this, I immediately began to quietly but sternly warn some "people" who were out there to **"<u>be aware</u>"** ...to **"<u>get ready!</u>"**

Now, I am sharing this dream/vision, believing that others like myself are beginning to have dreams and visions of the "End Times". If you are having any dreams/warnings, please consider sharing them so that we all can pray for understanding and "do" whatever it is that GOD may be telling us to do.

DREAM

February 25, 2015 (Morning)

There is a <u>long table</u> in a big, dark room of a house (?) Yet, there was "light" over the whole table area. I could see some vertical "light tunnels" within the dark background. There were donations/offerings on the table. I was standing behind the table ...

GOD gave me this dream/vision of a **long table** with offerings of "brokenness" from the people. **GOD was *pleased*** with this type of offering!

It wasn't the "people" that you could see; It was the "**offerings**" on the long table that they each brought (like a dish at a party) that pleased Him.

Praise GOD for the invitation of "brokenness" to His "Table of Sacrificial Offering"!

---

*Tonight: Our church is having a Special Anointed Prayer Service!... where people can "come up front" (Prayer Team) and have one of us pray with them!

*(The "table" was that "**area**" in <u>front</u> of all of us Prayer Warriors who were lined up along the front of the sanctuary. Some persons came up for prayer, **<u>broken</u>** and ready.)*

**Before I sat down, one of the ministers stopped me and the HOLY SPIRIT <u>confirmed</u> the dream between us, because the minister said to me, "HE is well pleased...GOD wants you to know that He is well pleased."

The <u>night</u> <u>before</u> GOD led me to read these scriptures:

Psalm 51:
-Purge me with hyssop, and I shall be clean: wash me, and I shall be whiter than snow. (vs7)

-Create in me a clean heart, O GOD; and renew a right spirit within me. (vs10)

-*The sacrifices of GOD are a* **broken spirit:** *a* _broken_ *and contrite heart, O GOD thou wilt not dispise. (vs17)*

AMEN!!!

DREAM

The Skinned Sheep

October 11, 2016

I wake up very early morn in the wee ours night from a most disturbing dream: I am outside in a cluttered area, like a junkyard. The scenery is very "grey". I am carrying around a **"skinned carcass"** of an animal on my outstretched forearms, searching ... looking for a place to put it. (I notice that the carcass' body was laying across my arms, with its back against me and the legs <u>outward</u>, towards/past my hands, The neck was drooped across my left arm and the tail area across my right arm. Somehow, I did not yet see pass the neck area to notice the animal's face; I was preoccupied with finding a place to put it.

*The carcass' meat was very clean, like clean, skinned chicken breast meat; no blood showing, no unclean wetness/mucus.

As I walked around, stepping through the clutter (junk?) on the ground, I look down on the ground to see a very small pink ***pig*** down by the right of me. It was just there, standing, facing me (my leg). This glimpse of the pig was brief and I seemed to be seeing the top of it from an elevated position. Suddenly, a "voice" from my left said that I need to **burn** it (the carcass that I was carrying). Then, I see a pail/bucket with a carcass (pig?) already ***in the pail***. I began placing the carcass in my arms over the pail/bucket to release it and just as I was dropping it into the bucket...*over* the other carcass already in it, I "see" the head of the animal; It was the head of a **lamb!** ... a perfectly skinned, perfect <u>lamb</u>! Oh, my! Suddenly, either I or *someone* **<u>"torched it"</u>**!

When I wake up, I jump out of the bed and go over to the sink to immediately begin washing my arms and hands!

I keep thinking, "LORD, what does this <u>mean</u>?

Prayer and Dream Research

Every day, all week, I would pray for the meaning and I would "tune in" for clues/answers:

First, I encountered the word "Apocalypse", meaning - uncovered/unveiled/revealed.

I then highlighted Key Markers in my dream for research:

1. Grey outside/cluttered ---- cluttered confounded sinful
   junkyard   world

2. Carrying a skinned   ---- skinned (revealed),
   carcass   exposed carry: Ministry/
                              responsibility

3. On my forearms   ---- I "handle the situation",
                              forbearing the problem.

4. Searching for a place ---- Seeking resolution/seeking purpose for the situation

5. Noticing the small pig ---- pig (sinner)

6. "Someone" said to <u>burn</u> it ---- Angel/GOD(?) instructing me what to do: <u>Burn</u>: sacrifice/ritual

7. I see a <u>pail</u> w/carcass in it ---- Pail: On 11/5/2016, I am led to read <u>Exodus 12:21,22,23</u> - Moses calls the elders to pick out a <u>lamb</u> to slaughter for the Passover animal. Drain the blood into a "**basin**"! ...

8. I put the **lamb** out of my arms into the pail...on top of the other carcass. ---- Lamb: innocent/believer/ blameless/ church/ gentle/humility...???

9. I/***Someone*** <u>torched</u> it! ---- Roasted sacrifice (Exodus 12:9)

DREAM

November 17, 2016

I see <u>shattered glass</u> all over the floor. Then, **a baby's leg (barefoot and bare)** is being "raised" towards me to get the glass out of the bottom of its foot. The child had been walking on the broken glass and now wanted to be relieved of the **glass in it's foot**. (I see <u>two</u> pieces: One on the <u>heel</u> and one in the <u>arch</u> area of the foot.) I then reach out to take the baby's leg to pull out the glass. (Oh yes. I didn't see any other part of the baby...only the leg and foot; the rest of him seemed invisible.)

Suddenly, I see **my face**, *big* in my vision; I could see inside my opened mouth that there was a piece of the shattered glass (cube?) at the middle (base) of my throat. I am about to "speak" with this glass particle at the base of my throat, at the back of my tongue!

Dream Research/Prayer

*Interpretation:

Baby -	New Christians; beginning; something in its fancy or early stages; innocent; dependent
Barefoot -	Humble before the presence of GOD
Feet -	A spiritual walk; heart attitude
Leg -	Walk, man's strength
Child's Leg -	(symbolic) relational interaction between us
Glass -	The destined time of man's life. His "glass" is run; a perspective glass (optic)

Mouth -	Instrument of witnessing (good or bad). Speaking evil or good words (warnings?); something from which come the issues of life; words coming against you.
Voice -	A message from GOD or satan; the Word of GOD; godly instruction.
Tongue -	Language, speech.

Chapter Three

JOURNAL ENTRIES (1997-TODAY)

*Winter (Dec) 1997:

It is very late tonight. I am upstairs in our bedroom. My husband is somewhere in the basement on his computer. I am watching TV and I am suddenly transfixed on this documentary about "wars" in the United States. I became upset and tearful as I watched how countries captured the Africans and brutally mistreated them...then, how the Jews were treated during the Holocaust...then, the Japanese... Chinese...Indians, etc. I was appalled at how we (Americans) lied, cheated, and deceived the Indians and massacred them, then forced them off their land into "ignorant" camps to degrade them and use them, just as they had done the Africans who were "taken" from their country.

I watched accounts of enslavement, murder, and malaise - to Jews...or "anyone" who was different! How prejudiced! How inhumane! How demonic! Why, LORD?

"Oh, LORD! We are still evil and deceptive, caring for no one or nothing but ourselves! We have not learned...we have not improved! Barbarians! We have failed You, LORD!" (Tears are now streaming down and I am visibly distraught to the point of near shock and despair.)

...What a night. What a revelation. What repentance in my heart for mankind! Something "happened" inside me tonight; This was the <u>beginning</u>...

(About a month or so later I had that "owl" dream...)

June 1998:

(5- 7th) - Weekend Retreat with a church.

(15-20) - Week in the Bahamas

(21st) - My mother-in-law passes away today, on *Father's Day.*

(27th) - Funeral; Afterwards, at home, I hear GOD say to me, *"No weapons formed against you will prosper".* (!!)

July 1998:

(2nd)   - Discipleship Class: A church leader confirms in the Spirit what GOD had said to me. Also, one of the deacons <u>shouted</u> with confirmation of this revelation because I had already told him <u>earlier</u> today that GOD had said, ***"No weapons formed against you will prosper."***

(20th)   - Before going to work this Monday morning, and after I prayed in tongues in the bathroom, GOD SAID: *"House is the place to love, to love."* GOD also called me *"Beloved"*! "Bless the LORD - Bless His Holy Name!" I <u>sing</u> to GOD in tongues! Wow!

*During this summer, GOD began telling me to put **7 potatoes** (must be 7) in every bag to give out to people. One of the church ushers provided me with **"Roman Road"** scriptures on a flyer. Also, I heard someone testify on the radio how GOD provided them with the words, **"GOD loves you right where you are, but He loves you too much to let you stay there"**. Subsequently, I found myself preparing for evangelism: I started asking co-workers, family, and friends to not throw away their grocery bags, but to give them to me.

I then made flyers for evangelism. I started with 50lb bags of potatoes, placing 7 potatoes, along with the flyers in each plastic grocery bag. I would then go out to the "uttermost" of neighborhoods and hand them out door-to-door and to people passing by. I was amazed at the reception and rewards from this ministry! People who were too oppressed or preoccupied to be "bothered" by a piece of paper would suddenly view those flyers through different eyes because of the **potatoes**. They would say, "Thank you", Bless you", and they would smile...and you <u>knew</u> that GOD would do the rest!

"LOOK...AND WATCH...BE UTTERLY ASTOUNDED! FOR I WILL WORK A WORK IN YOUR DAYS WHICH YOU WOULD NOT BELIEVE..." Habakkak 1:5 (NKJV)

After reading a magazine, these words reached out to me; "Walk in wisdom toward those who are outside, redeeming the time." Do it urgently! Make the best possible use of your time.

August 1998:

(12th) - Listening to the radio, ***"Go! Spread the Word... Now!!"*** I pray w/kids before school and I talk about how GOD is moving in your life <u>each</u> <u>day</u>. Discern GOD's mission for you: Pray - Notice confirmation around you - Notice people sent around you. (...In accordance with Word or scripture?)

(15th) - Morn before going to work: *"Hold the baby"... CHRIST...Pray...Do...and I will...CHRIST... Hold...<u>Hold</u> her...CHRIST...if you don't... (jumbled sentence)"*

(17th) - Morn before work; *"Hold...Pray...CHRIST... Hold on...CHRIST is the way...the right... Praise Him...My darling...He is LORD...is my Father... the right...try <u>hard</u>...Praise...do the right...try Him...Hold..."*

(22nd) - We graduate from Discipleship class today.

(24th) - Monday (Day off) *"...Praise Him...Christian... Hold Him in your heart......Please ...change."* Mom and I go out to eat. She stays awhile.

September 1998:

(11th) - (I am **ushering** during this week's neighborhood revival). Pastor told us at last night's revival to 'bring a sinner the next night'. So, on the way to church, I notice a bar club. Then I pulled onto the parking lot and convinced an older man to follow me in his car to my church. (*I'm sure that he really followed me for reasons that had <u>nothing</u> to do with GOD.*) Now, the "neighborhood" revival was held outside, on the grounds in front of the church. The man stayed until another usher discouraged him, noticing that he was "a bit under the weather", so he left halfway through the sermon.

That night, the HOLY SPIRIT wakes me up and has me <u>praising</u> <u>GOD</u>!

(12th) - *Today is the **first time** that I do **"<u>Potatoes and Prayers</u>"**

Evangelism for my GOD. Also, today GOD led me to read the scripture, Romans 10:9 ***"That if thou confess with thy***

mouth the LORD JESUS, and believe in thou heart that GOD has raised Him from the dead, thou shalt be saved."

- Later tonight (Saturday), I usher again for the revival week. They used that <u>same</u> scripture on the pulpit!

October 1998:

(2nd) - Morning prayer before work; "...serve your mother...serve your sister...serve your brother... He is my Father...JESUS is LORD...tomorrow... strive...start...change...tomorrow...seven..."

-At work today, my coworker and friend informs me that his recently deceased mother touched him and his brother. He said that a "blue light" followed him.

(12th) - Morning (Holiday*): "...It is starting... 40 in days...David, David, Paul...call in the LORD... Cry in the LORD...<u>Hold</u> in the LORD...Praise in the LORD...Sing in the LORD. It's the LORD."*

(18th) - Prayers: "...Stay in the LORD...Cry in the LORD... in 17 days...Praise the LORD...in 17 days...in 17 days! (in <u>strong</u> voice)...it's alright...time..."special".*

(21st) - Woke up in the wee hours with a dire urge to pray for my niece. I placed my hand on her forehead and began praying for her <u>soul</u> in CHRIST. The HOLY SPIRIT took over in the prayers.

November 1998:

(10th) - During night prayers & meditation: "...7 (seven)...time...taking in the night...taking him...someone is the light...JESUS is the light...GOD is good, is good, is good...change him...saving in the LORD...<u>Stay Here</u>...GOD is right."

(11th) - Bible Study; I received verbal rejection from someone. (?!)

(19th) - I gave out **"Potatoes and Prayers"** this evening as I visit Mom.

December 1998:

(18th) - "Pride"...change it...Stay here in the LORD...

save in the LORD....Praise Him...Changing in the LORD..."Signs".

(24th) - I visit **Mr. "Robert"** at the Nursing Home; After the visit, on my way out to my car... just before I get to the door, I feel the LORD stop me and lead me around to a room with a black lady in bed, seemingly in an immobile (coma?) state. I am urged to pray for her at the foot of her bed. She then <u>sits up</u>, still asleep and faces **up** towards the ceiling for a few minutes. Then she lays back down. (I <u>thank</u> the LORD, JEHOVAH!)

*November 1998 - February 01, 1999:** I experience mistreatment at work.

Feb 02, 1999 - Smelling <u>victory</u>! Praise GOD! GOD is already working it out!

January 1999:

(2nd) - **Dream:** Heavy rain. I am in my car, traveling in heavy downtown traffic and in heavy rain. I am driving on a street along the harbor where I can see the harbor on my right. (*I seem to be heading towards South Baltimore direction.*) Now, as I am near the harbor, I have a *choice* of driving to the left… away from the harbor along with the other cars, but instead, I stayed in the right lane by the harbor. Then, I pulled over and got out of my car (still in the heavy rain) and began walking towards the harbor pier to "talk" to JESUS (?) (Can't see a face.) standing out there. As I am walking towards JESUS, I look over to the left and see a **small rowboat** on *turbulent* waters and I say something to JESUS (in the spirit) about not desiring to get into that little boat on such waters. [End of dream] *When I awake, I am spiritually hugged and comforted by JESUS.

(2nd) - (Messages during prayer) …crying in Him… Praise! …Tell everybody …CHRIST…saving in the LORD… somebody else…sorry in the night …Somebody crying in the night…calling in the night ...saving him ...Stay here...saving in the LORD. Tell everybody (He's my Father) Special ...changing in the LORD...shining in the night...saving in the night...crying in the night...shining in the night ...tomorrow is the LORD...It's so hard in the LORD. Special... changing...crying in the night...change in the night.

January 1999 (cont.):

(16) - Usher Meeting - I am assigned to do "Patronage" for Ushers' Anniversary.

"Stay, strive...Put it in the Name (of the LORD) ...Save ... STAND... PRIZE STAND... Tell them, everybody...Somebody here crying in the night ... Tomorrow!

(17) - I did **8 bags** of "Potatoes and Prayer" in Seton Apts. after 11 o'clock service.

(26) - Morning Prayers: "Stay here...Stand...Seven... Taste the LORD...Praise ...Stand...Save... Somebody here...Somebody crying in the

night ...Somebody here in the LORD...
Pray ...Saving him...Praise ...Stay in the
LORD ...is good." *Led to read Jeremiah 50 -
(Judgment Against Babylon)

(30) - I visit Mom; I give out **10 bags** of **"Potatoes and prayers"** in her area. Back home, a neighbor stops by to get my niece tonight; After praying for me, she exclaimed, "You're a <u>warrior</u>!"

  - I visit **Mr. "Robert"** at the Nursing Home: Mr. Robert was a <u>very</u> large black man whose room was across the hall from my mother-in-law's room. (She passed on in June.) Now, he was blind and <u>feared</u> by all the nursing staff. But, the HOLY SPIRIT had drawn me across the hall to him as he played his radio very loudly. Whenever I would come into his room, he would calm down and smile and speak with me with the highest respect like a <u>child</u> to his dear mother. The staff was amazed. We talked and sang and discussed GOD. (He was from a loving, religious home, but had rebelled and lived a maleficent life in the dark, street world.) Now struck blind from deadly illness, Mr. "Robert" would lash out at all the staff...except when I would visit with him. Later, GOD had placed it on my heart to leave instructions for the family to keep the radio tuned to a Christian station when he becomes too weak to refuse.

Mr. "Robert" returned to GOD before he died.

February 1999:

(01) - Mailed out my papers: Open spiritual attack. (GOD had led me to anoint areas with holy water...water that <u>He</u> made holy!)

(02) - News of victory!

(07) - I tell Sunday School and a minister about "Potatoes and Prayers"/(No response)

(08 - I tell Women's Support Group. (no one interested.)

(09) - I tell my friend about the potato ministry. -- She wishes to help right away!

(15) - (Holiday) - HOLY SPIRIT speaks all morning. (My husband hears me in bed.)

"Seven...change...Somebody here in the LORD...SAVING him...He hears you......He hears me...in the LORD is good."

- F A S T I N G Week -

March 1999:

(08) - I praise the LORD this morning and <u>sing</u> in the LORD. I pray for the church and the Pastor and his family.

*Later this month...

The church was given a <u>truck load</u> of fresh sweet potatoes from a farmer. Our Pastor announced that anyone can take sweet potatoes home. Yet, few people took any. So, after asking for them, I got someone with a truck and we loaded the sweet potatoes onto it. **FREE potatoes for the ministry!!!**

(13)   - **I change my food fast** to "Holy Oil and Face-wash and Prayer" (personal). The HOLY SPIRIT helps me (in agreement) with my <u>private</u> ritual.

Message after ritual: Ephes. 4&5, *...ye walk worthy of the vocation of which ye are called... walk not as other Gentiles walk, in the vanity of their mind...walk in love. ..walk as children of light...have no fellowship with the unfruitful works of darkness.*

April 1999:

(05)   - A friend and I do **Potatoes and Prayers** (with the sweet potatoes!) until 9 PM in her neighborhood.

May 1999:

(05)   - *Led to read:* PROVERBS 7. "Keep My words and lay up My commandments with thee. **Keep My commandments** and LIVE; and My law as the apple of thine eye. Bind them with thy

fingers, write them upon the table of thine heart."

(08)   ***My son got married today in our back yard. (Lovely, blessed ceremony)**

(16)   -   **I have a "<u>dream</u>" this morning:** (Rows of seats) White room - I sit in the back row (section) with the paraplegic people. Then, I go up towards the near front section of seats and I see two women in middle row. I begin rebuking the one lady about using (holding up) seats with her belongings. Then, I admonish her friend for excusing her wrong behavior. Next, I see a long white table with cases of boxed food, etc <u>neatly</u> placed on the tables.(Offerings?) Suddenly, I notice that I have a <u>wrong</u> donation in my hands ...a <u>partially</u> filled pot of greens!

*Now I know that I should first get rid of that "big" log in my own eye before trying to pluck splinters from another's eye. Stop judging! <u>Only GOD judges</u>. Whew! **(My offering was 'lacking'!)**

(23) - 6 AM - I pray and cry to JESUS for not being fruitful and for disobeying.

JESUS said, "Take My hand and cry in the LORD". I did. Then, He had me to read Jeremiah 33 (Promises of Peace and Prosperity) ...not because I cried, but because it is in GOD's plan.

June 1999:

(04) - **Retreat** - Elizabethtown, PA. college with another church (weekend retreat).

(06) - **<u>DREAM</u>**: Shapes of little **children** all around me! They shine like lightbulbs.

In my dream, they are not strangers...I knew them!.. (I am to <u>teach</u> them... a **Children's Ministry!?**)

(08) - Evening Prayer in garage: "...saving...changing... show Me! ...<u>Chosen</u> ...choose to the <u>right</u>! Take the <u>right</u>! ...chosen."

(09) - Morning..."Tell them My stories...striving... changing...praising...SAVE! <u>Tell</u> <u>them</u>."

Around this time I was compelled to buy musical instruments for the children, school supplies, Biblical visual aids, old school desks and chairs...and my basement began to take on a "new" look.

(15) - 4 AM - Woke up: "...Sending someone to help you." ...choose to the right! chosen...light... JESUS is the light."

(22) - Morn: Joshua 11

(23) - Morn: Ruth 3

July 1999:

(08) - Woke up (5 AM?); The HOLY SPIRIT is with me. Last summer, I had started with **50 lb** bags of potatoes. Then, on this Thursday, July 08, 1999, after my morning prayer time, I got these messages from the HOLY SPIRIT:

"Taste the LORD. The LORD is the light...the right...Take My hand...Stand in the light...chosen...GOD hears you... saving...seven, seven...Goodness is...Praise Him...**Ten times**

Ten... Save, My dear...changing...changing...To the right! Taste the LORD, My FATHER; HE's right... Forty."

*When I reflected back on **"Ten times ten"**, I knew that I needed to increase the amount of potatoes to 100 lbs! ...50 lbs always went <u>too</u> <u>fast</u>! (So I began to buy two 50 lb bags.)

Scripture: Micah 6:7,8 --The LORD has already told you what is good; To do what is right, to love mercy, and to walk humbly with the LORD."

(10) - In my room to pray: Led to read Mark 2&3. (Don't need to wait for training to do GOD's work right away.) The Sabbath was made to benefit people, not people to benefit the Sabbath. Fasting/How can Satan cast out Satan?

August 1999:

(20) - Bought potatoes from church member/farmer.
*Potatoes went up from $9 to $<u>15</u>!! (50lbs.)

September 1999:

> Ms. Naomi, another friend, and myself begin Saturday classes at Howard University School of Divinity.

December 1999:

> I have the <u>first</u> Sunday School in my home with my niece and grandchildren.

January 2000:

(14) - Woke up at 4 AM - Feeling a drift away from my LORD. Led to read:

Nehemiah in my Study Bible; GOD has a vision for us. There are "walls" that we need to build. (Prayer)

(15) - My friend and I do Potatoes and Prayers in "The Village". She and I feel truly blessed by GOD for choosing us to spread the gospel in such a loving and profound way.

(16) - Around 5AM: I am downstairs, sitting on the couch by the light near the fireplace writing while everyone is asleep.

"...I so much love you...I will save you...I <u>chose</u> you... Change your heart...I so much love you...My child...GOD hears you...pray, pray, pray ... It's alright ...I so much love you...It's alright in the light."

...STRIVE FOR CONSISTENCY/ OBEDIENCE EACH DAY...

(27) - Spiritual friend and I are scheduled to see the pastor at her church; HOLY SPIRIT! Yes!!! Spiritual Confirmation!

February 2000:

*(01) - My son's "trouble". (Remembering GOD's message to me, "Trust Me.")

(15) - **"7...7...7...7...7... in days ... so much love ... 7 ...charge him ... I stand in you ...7... It's alright ... pray ...praise Him ... start now."**

(22) - I do Potatoes and Prayers: I give flyers to some girls on a H.S. lot. One gay girl thought her life was too dirty for GOD to love her; She kept saying, "GOD loves <u>me</u>? Hey, yall!... GOD <u>loves</u> me!" Then, she said, "Now I guess I have to go to church. But I can never go to church... not with my lifestyle." Then I told her, "What does that <u>paper</u> say? ... **GOD loves you, right where you <u>are</u>!**" She looked at the paper and studied it. Suddenly, she began saying to the other girls..."GOD <u>loves</u> me!" (Amen.)

* I fast for seven (7) days.

* This month, I taught my grandchildren, my niece and nephews in the basement: We sang, danced, and played instruments. We also dressed up to dramatize characters in the Bible. I enjoyed it! I loved it! Oh, the blessings of GOD!

March 2000:

(04) - A Christian friend from my niece's school does 1st Bible Study session with the kids in my basement.

(16) - Prayer: **"...Now you know...Heaven and earth...7 days...7 years...I save you... GOD hears you..."**

     - Led to read: Proverbs 3:21 (Seek Wisdom)

(29) - Potatoes and Prayers in the city.

(30) - Woke up at 3/4 AM: Led to go to the floor and pray...for <u>all</u>. Must pray for the world, friends, family and myself.

     - Led to read: **Matthew 24 - End times has <u>begun</u>.** Spread the word ... Do the Potatoes and Prayers.

April 2000:

(01) - Woke up early; "Pray, pray"

(13) - First time Potatoes and Prayers combined with an Apostolic church! (After work, 12 people, 6:45-7:45PM) - We do Evangelism together.

(20) - Potatoes and Prayers with Apostolic church again for evangelism on streets.

(22) - Picked up potatoes from a church member (3 bags). Then, gave out Potatoes at a location sent to by the LORD. (Blessed!) I met a lady in front of a market; she had needed (wanted) <u>potatoes</u> for her breakfast but didn't have enough money to get them.

(25) - Visited Rev. Gray; I told him about my "wilderness walk" and the potato ministry. He truly understood and he gave me encouraging words.

(28) - Appointment with Pastor and Discipleship teacher: GOD opens a door for potatoes ministry!

(30) - **"...My child...GOD hears you...The SAVIOR knows you...Heaven and earth knows your name...I have your name(?) ...Stay...Hear... Taste the LORD...My time is here...The time is right...Changing your heart...Seven is right...Now you know... Walk in the light ...Pray in the light... JESUS is GOD ... saving you."**

May 2000:

(02) - <u>HOLY SPIRIT</u> woke me up around 3AM - pulled me out of the bed to the floor to pray...in tongues, on my face, arms stretched out...Then my hands together in prayer... praying <u>hard</u>!!? Then, I slide back into bed.

(04) - **"...Send him to Me... Send him...He stays here...You know... I hear you ...Tuesday."**

(07) - Sunday: Went to Sunday School at my church. I felt led to "get up" from the 11:00 Service (Substitute preacher) and I went to the Apostolic church. A member came over to me and said, "You're in the right place." You did the right thing. You are where you are supposed to be right now. Let it go.

Everything is happening as it should." ... and I never <u>told</u> her anything!

(12) - I go to <u>Howard University</u> for Commencement Ceremony - My certificate.

(13) - "...Change you...Who is your Father? ...Who's child are you? ...Now you know... Teach you... Sunday is a "special" day. It's alright... changing...Will put it in your heart.

(13) - Sudden black storm; **Lightning** hit the **tree** in front of the garage and sliced 1/3 of it and it fell across the driveway. (*Before this, I had been praying to GOD to cast any lingering demons around/in our home into the trees!*)

June 2000:

(02) - **Retreat!** Weekend retreat with Apostolic church.

(07) - "...couldn't ...you... light ...(I)? change your time... (I) change your name... I (have)? your heart... Me your hand...strive."

(08) - Prayer (In garage): "...saving... changing... show Me!... <u>Chosen</u>... choose to the <u>right</u>! Take the <u>right</u>! ... Chosen."

(09) - Prayer time with GOD this AM: "**...Tell them My stories... stories... striving, changing... praising... SAVE! ...Tell them.**"

July 2000:

(07) - "**...Glory to GOD...Praise ...Charge him(?)... Recite(?) to him... Pray...TUESDAY is alright... TUESDAY... JESUS is GOD ...GOD heard your name seventeen times! HE knows you... SEVENTEEN! ...couldn't change your time...GOD changes. JESUS chose you! ...Loves you...Heaven and Earth... GOD, Changing your time (Good News) ...So much love in your heart. GOD changing ...SAVE you...So much love.**"

(11) - "**GOD hears you now... Keep hearing your name... changing...Hear you...Knows you... GOD changes... couldn't change your time... GOD changing...Taste the LORD... chose you... JESUS chose you... Knows your heart...chosen, chosen... Talk right...Your**

name...SEVEN TIMES your name... GOD heard your name seven times... your name... Change your light... changing... time... every day... Somebody knows you... Keep hearing you... charge him... send him."

(12) - "Plan to cry."

(18) - Awake in bed 4:30 AM; **HOLY SPIRIT/JESUS here.**

"...Couldn't take her...It's alright...4 days ...The time is right...JESUS hears your name...JESUS, putting charge over you... Chose you for hope...Praise the LORD... Pray...Put charge in you for hoping...Take every day...<u>Send</u> Him...Put charge in Him... Who chose...changing...changing your name ... GOD hears you...calls you...Paul (?) hears you...<u>GOD</u> chose you...Put hope in you...<u>Changing</u> you...Do you <u>hear</u> Me?!"

(21) - Reverend and her kids help bag potatoes; do flyers. Five 50 lb bags!

(29)　-　At Bible Study: Reverend's neighbor will get me Bibles and help me get Lighthouse door knockers. Reverend tells me that Pastor will financially support Potatoes and Prayers ministry! GREAT-T! BLESSED!!

July 2000:

(30)　-　At 9:45 AM, I go and talk to Reverend about Potatoes and Prayers, Apostolic evangelism combining with our ministry and about taking my family to the Apostolic church and being filled with the HOLY SPIRIT; about GOD slaying me (us) in the SPIRIT when three of us met at a home to discuss our ministries.

This same afternoon, my husband and I go to the Apostolic service; My son and daughter-in-law meet us there. I tell GOD, "I send him (my son) to you." After service, their pastor tells me, "Yes, stay in Him...live through Him!"

* As we were leaving service, I get stopped by outstretched arms from a nice lady and I am then given a message by yet

another woman that she was hugging. -This woman began saying:

"GOD wants me to tell you that your test of faith is over. I have brought you through the refining coals and you have come out <u>victorious</u>. Not by anything that I have done in you, but by your <u>FAITH</u> and <u>standing</u> have you endured the trials. And I want you to know right now, on <u>this</u> <u>day</u>, that it is over and that I Am well pleased. You are my child...chosen. You are now stronger in your faith. Know that I <u>alone</u> did this for you; Test you...mold you. I love you, my child. I Am proud of you. (Trust in Me <u>alone</u> ...Walk in <u>Me</u>!) Sometimes you thought you may never see the victory in what was before you. Some nights you thought you might be loosing your mind. Know that everything you may not overcome, that I will make everything alright. Know that it is <u>done</u>! I have my protection over you...No one will harm you...And know that when you overcome, that there is blessing and reward afterwards."

August 2000:

(05) - AM Prayers: **"...4 times I hear your name...7 chances...So much love."**

    - Read: Jeremiah 35-40 (The Faithful Recabites). Obey GOD and do not part from it! Keep His laws!)

(10) - **"Charge...chances...Pray...Test... Can't you see?... Take every day... changing... 7 ... charging... It's alright... I <u>hear</u> you. Your <u>name</u>."**

*(13) - **"Vision"** while leaving Norfolk, VA around 2 AM. (pulpit/tall candles)

(23) - **"In 7 years...I love you... JESUS is GOD... chances... Can't you see... 4 times... I save you... changing your name... It's alright... HE is here... Pray... strive... GOD keeps hearing you... <u>Special</u>... so much Love... He <u>chose</u> you... Praise the LORD!! PRAISE HIM!"**

(26) - **"Feast"**: GOD had been telling me over and over to have a "feast"! (What feast, LORD?) Then,

finally I decided I would have a cookout. GOD had also shown me in the scriptures to go unto the uttermost and invite strangers to the feast:

<u>Matthew 22: 8,9</u> (Wedding Feast invitation) *⁸ "Then he said to his slaves, The wedding is ready, but those who were invited were not worthy. ⁹" Go therefore to the main highways, and as many as you find there, invite to the wedding feast.' ¹⁰ "Those slaves went out into the streets and gathered together all they found, both evil and good; and the wedding hall was filled with dinner guests.*

When I saw that the invited friends did not come, I immediately asked my nephew and his invited schoolmate to "follow me" in his schoolmate's car to wherever GOD leads me... to locate the people (strangers) to the cookout that GOD told me about. My nephew's friend was a Christian teen who did not question me, but followed behind my car into town until I "felt" where I was to stop! We "saw" a woman sitting on her porch; next door to her was a man and children playing in the front yard. I shared my story with them and they all came ... believing! But the woman on her porch also said to me, "Wait, my mother is in the house and I think she will come. Well, when that elderly woman come out barely walking without assistance, I "knew" she was the one GOD wanted me to bring! There was just something so special about her appearance. This elderly woman began to remark how she <u>loved</u> GOD and how she was so grateful for the invite.

Now, as we drove these strangers in our two cars towards my house, I noticed others on their porches with kids playing and I stopped and told them about what GOD asked me to do. Then, a <u>grandmother</u> believed me to the point that she actually sent her grandchildren with us ...without even getting my name or number!

Needless to say, we had a grand time at the cookout with plenty of food that GOD had privileged me to purchase in preparation; The kids played, the people ate, and when the elderly lady (bent over) told me that she was in her house without food because she had to spend her money on her medicine, I then realized that the packaged chicken in the crates where for <u>her</u>! I packed her grocery bags of food and we had prayer in my living room and we had **a HOLY GHOST time!**

When I took the "grandchildren" back, the grandmother was upset with herself because she realized that she had sent those kids off with me without identification! I then too realized how GOD can prepare the hearts of those whom He calls... whom He <u>invites</u>!

After this encounter, the elderly lady and I became closer than she and her own daughters and I began to care for her. Soon I noticed that she was sharing food with the man next door to her who was in need. Thus, I also started bringing food to them both. Over time, jealousy rose up in her daughters and they began to "compete" with me in caring for their mother. Once they "got the message" in caring for their own mother, they resumed taking good care of her. Then, I was 'weaned' away. But, before I left, the elderly lady gave her life to CHRIST and joined the church which was only blocks away from where she lived. Wow! Look at what my GOD can do!

<u>Matthew 22:2-5</u> *

<u>²**The kingdom of heaven is like a certain king, which**</u> <u>**made a marriage for his son,**</u> ³And **sent forth** his servants to <u>call</u> <u>them</u> that were **bidden** to the wedding: and <u>they</u> <u>would not come.</u> ⁴Again, he sent forth other servants, saying Tell them which are bidden, **Behold, I have prepared my dinner:** my oxen and fatlings are killed, and all things are ready: come unto the marriage. ⁵**But they made light of it, and went their ways**, one to his farm, another to his merchandise...

September 2000:

    (06)   -   **"Follow Me... Follow Me... (Speak) Peace... Pressed Down... PRAY...Glory... JESUS hears you... Your light... chances... JESUS is LORD... The LORD hears your heart... TIME (Spend) in the LORD."**

    (09)   -   **I call Mr. Roche (Farmer) to tell him I can't make it this morning for gleaning help (apples) at his farm. ...so sad.**

October 2000:

(14) - **"Plan" your light...cleanse your heart.**

(18) - **"Why are you crying? ...Feast!!"** ...I then get up off the floor and I go downstairs to eat my dinner! ...even meat! ...and dessert! Here, I realized that GOD was answering my prayers. He was *"Taking him... saving him."* GOD was changing my son!

You see, I had been crying for my only begotten son...in trouble. But now I understand that the answer to our prayers may not come the way we think; that GOD's ways are not our ways...**But, GOD's ways are <u>always</u> best!**

"Bless the LORD, O my soul! Bless His Holy Name!"

(20) - **"PLAN ...PLAN!" "...sees planning...sees changing...choose you... for sure...."**

(22 - **"At just the right time, I will respond... Take the gospel <u>out</u>...."**

(24) - I go to court 1st time with him.

(25) - This morning I'm led to read Isaiah 31. - <u>Don't</u> go to organization to solicit help! Trust <u>GOD</u>!

When I get to court, I show them the scripture; I tell them I'm not going with them for the appointment with the organization. *We all prayed in a circle outside of the courtroom. (*They left court around 10AM and came back around 3:30 PM with several organization members.*) Oh, no!!!

Lies!!! - Defenders <u>sleeping</u>! - <u>Terrible</u> day in court!!!!
(This just <u>can't</u> be happening before my eyes!)

(29) - [Sunday] -This morning, much prayer; much relationship with the HOLY SPIRIT...with JESUS.

I go to an **Apostolic Church**; ...on <u>FIRE</u> with the HOLY SPIRIT!! HOLY! HOLY!! HOLY!! ...Yes!!! - As you know, I go up front.

Dance! Dance! Dance! ...in the SPIRIT! The Pastor takes my hand. O, HOLY SPIRIT!

He says, "No weapons formed against you shall prosper! ...The Joy of the LORD is your strength! ...You have the power!" - I dance, up front; dance, dance, <u>dance</u>! What a time! Blessed LORD and SAVIOR!

* I later used GOD's tithes to buy dinners (Soul Food) for the elderly lady (I've been assigned to take care of her.) and her neighbor, and one for my <u>mom</u>.

November 2000:

(10) - 6 AM Morn Prayer: **"Pray, Pray"** ... **"Peace in the light...Peace on earth..."7 years your love." "Please take care of it" ...(??) Changing you today. Who's Special? Chosen you...take care of you. Peace in the earth...JESUS hears you...So Special is the LORD in you."**

(12) - Morn: (Waking up) **"Buy a ticket!"** (...what??) Then, when I take the elderly lady to my church,

Pastor announces they were selling "Tickets" for a breakfast next Saturday. I buy a ticket for me and the elderly lady.

(18) - Church "Unity Day" breakfast at 9AM - Excellent! **The elderly lady says that she's going to join the church tomorrow!**

(19) - [Sunday] - I take the elderly lady to church. She goes up front and she **joins** the church! I then leave to go with my husband to a baseball game at the stadium.

(26) - The elderly lady does not go to church today. She asked me to <u>please</u>, please pray for her. Our Sunday school class prays for her.

(26) - Morn Prayer: **"Beloved is your name." (My name!) ...Be careful in your love... Wait on the LORD...Be still ...PRAY ...Change is coming ...JESUS has your number...Behave in the LORD."**

December 2000:

(01) - I go to prayer service at church tonight: GOD is in the house! (HE speaks...through my mouth!) "People ...calling you ... Cleansing you...."

(02) - Morning prayer: **"Special ...GOD's love in you ...Be standing ...be changing... HE stands in you...Take care of you... "People love you, says JESUS." ...People will hear you...CHRIST the LORD ...He's calling in the LORD is GOD ...Be loving in Him ...Be <u>careful</u> in your love... Be <u>sure</u> in the LORD... GOD shows you, My dear... Be praying... Be saving ...Peace in the light... Be careful of your love. JESUS hears your name. Be saving in you ...I stand in you ...I so much love you ... Peace in the light ...taste better ... <u>Behave</u> in the LORD...Be still...I'm taking you to the Right...Be still...7 years your love."**

(03) - Woke up with: **"...church needs to get on their knees."** Note: Why on the knees? **"...because... pray."**

(11) - Morning prayer; Led to read: <u>Job 5,6,7</u> **"...Be strong... Be very strong... Be still ...<u>Watch</u> Me!"**

Verdict time: I go to court; ... A **black day** for us all!!! Woe is me ...my son!...my son! My GOD... My just GOD...my tears...Yet, my thanks to GOD...my hope, still... my sorrow!! Our <u>pain</u>....

(13) - Morning prayer: **"...Cleanse ... be close to Him... Be so close to Him ...changing ...chances ...cast down ... chances... chosen ...Be close to Him ...couldn't tell you ...JESUS changes ...strive ...PRAY...PRAY...Believe...."**

(14) - Prayers: **"Be loving... Beloved is your name ...I stand in you ...changing ... Hearing your name is good ...JESUS gave you your name ...Be careful in your love ...close to Me ...I care for you ...chosen."**

(27) - Prayer: **"...Cleanse ...I love you ...Be a soldier ...Be strong."**

(28) - Morn: **"Your name ...changing ...cleansing ...chose your love in Him ...Be your name, Beloved. GOD's love in you."**

January 2001:

(07) - I wake up; feeling closer to GOD, loving to be closer to Him.

(10) - Morning prayer; **"Be strong, be very strong. Be a <u>soldier</u>...so strong. Be a loving girl. Be loving. GOD has your number. Glory to the LORD! GOD hears you. JESUS is changing you. Glory Hallelujah! Be loving, my baby! ...Be a soldier. I'm with you. Be close to your number...'Be a saving'."**

*Led to read: Psalm 20 (Praising GOD for victory in battle.) Trust GOD for deliverance, not man or weaponry, but in <u>worship</u>. (<u>GOD</u>'s power is what's behind the weaponry!)

(11)   -   Morning Prayer: **"I love you, Beloved. Trust Me. It's alright. It's alright. Be strong. Be saving. I am with you."**

(12)   -   Morning prayer: **"<u>HE</u> says to you: 'Be a saving'... I am here... Be a soldier... Be a soldier... I am with you... Be strong... GOD hears you... Close to you... TRUST Me ... TRUST ME... chosen."**

*Read: *"Someone's"* book (Led to pick it up): The page is already opened to:

"When the last days come, I will give My SPIRIT to everyone. Yet another page states, "I will always see the LORD near me, and I will not be afraid with Him at my right side."

(12)   -   2nd Morning prayer: **"Thank You! Bless your Holy Name!"**

                  "Be saving... Be loving... Be careful... JESUS hears you... cleansing in the night... JESUS hears you... changing you."

(14) - Prayer - **"Be strong...Be close to ME... Be saving...be loving...so much love in you... Be careful in your love...cleansing...changing you... Be a <u>soldier</u>."**

(14) - 8 AM Service and Sunday School: Message; *<u>Let loose</u>* my grieving/holding over my son. Sinful when we forget that <u>GOD</u> is in control and that we should Trust Him ...always. (Get back in focus so GOD can use me.) Stop trying to reclaim duty to <u>save</u> my family; remember that GOD already <u>told</u> me to let go, that He <u>has</u> it! ...that He has <u>everyone</u>!

(20) - Gleaning Day! Sweet potatoes and apples. (For evangelizing!)

(21) - I give out some apples and potatoes; Ms. Naomi tells me she dreamed of *fire in 4 homes! We <u>pray</u>.

(23) - Morn: **"...Be TOLD...Be chosen...I love you... For your love is GOD..."**

Tonight, I pray with all the adults in the house. On my door: *"In This House, We Will Serve The LORD"*.

(24) - ***FIRE!!!** - I went to get food for dinner while my husband cooked French fries; He left the cooking oil unattended and the stove caught fire and burned the cabinets. The fire truck was at my home when I returned! Everyone was safe! Whew! "Thank YOU, LORD!"

February 2001:

(02) - 4/5 AM? - Woke up talking: **"...Trust Me, trust Me...Be strong, trust Me... Take care of the children... Be close to Me...Trust...."**

(03) - Morn: **"Trust Me...My beloved...I take care of you...so strong in you..."**

(11) - At an Apostolic church: Told, "You'll be getting more people to bring to CHRIST. GOD <u>loves</u> you. You are blessed."

(17) - I go "gleaning".

(23) - **"TRUST ME!" "HE favors you...Be holy in the LORD...Be strong...Be a soldier!"**
(Concern for my son during this time.)

(28) - **"Passed your trial. Just TRUST in JEHOVAH. GOD hears you."** ...Be taking care...Be a soldier...called...Be strong in HIM." ...trials."

March 2001:

(01) - Morn: **"GOD hears you." "Give Him something...Give Him <u>something</u>."**

To myself: *What, LORD???* Then, I see the "Daily Bread" booklet for February 28. (It's easier to give things than to give <u>ourselves</u>.) Deny myself? ...what, LORD? I look down and see "criticism". --Wow! GOD really knows what I need to give up...and to give it to <u>HIM</u>!! (Give up criticism! ...Yes, LORD! I will try...<u>Hard</u>!

(04) - **"Just <u>TRUST</u> ME...I love you...for talking it...for... I told you...Beloved...I believe in you...The love I give in you. The Body is JEHOVAH...The Body is JEHOVAH.**

Be loving...Be strong...The Babies...for TALKING in the LORD."

(11) - "Until you know, until you see, until you trust... Take care of yourself ...can't be for everyone...I care about you...so close to you... so far from Me... 7 years, your love... "Bow down! Bow Down!"

*Thank You, my loving GOD! (I have tried <u>all</u> weekend to please everyone else.) My merciful FATHER!

April 2001:

(01) - AM Prayers: "Love your husband"... JESUS...Be loving...Be glorious ... TRUST JEHOVAH."

**Preparing and buying/choosing items for our "kitchen" to upgrade from insurance coverage from the <u>fire</u>.

"...ten, ten, ten..." (30?) (...30 what?)

"Be careful in your love..." "I chose you...I trust you...MY love in you. ...trice, trice, trice..." (??)

(12) - Baby Shower. Cook out. My second grandson!

"...trice, trice, trice...."

June 2001:

(01) - Reverend and I leave for **Retreat** at 8:30 AM on a bus to Elizabethtown, PA. Y-E-S-S!! On the way there, while still on the bus, Reverend says GOD gave her the name for the church she was to start!

July 2001:

(01) - Sunday: **Reverend's <u>church</u> had its first service!**

(09) - Prayers *..."trice, trice, trice"*

(11) - Morn: Prayers - *"...The time is right ...Be strong ...I love you ...The time is right ...Be Holy ...The body is holy ...changing ...."*

*BABY is born! My second grandson! Praise GOD!

(15) - I read in a **Magazine**: *"When GOD wants to bring more power into your life, He brings more pressure."*

(22) - Baby's Dedication today.

August 2001:

(03) - Good News! - Reverend gets **installed as pastor** of her church today. Bad News -...Deep and shattering tears.

(05) - My granddaughter and another girl get baptized today!

(31) - Prayer - ...*"Ten, ten. ten."*

September 2001:

(01) - Morning prayer; *"10,10,10" ...Trust Me and I will change your heart. Just trust Me. ...The babies trust Me...Peace all over you..."*

(While on week's vacation in VA.)

September 2001 continued:

(02)   -   Back from vacation: *

1. Sister crying
2. Lady #1 - son paralyzed on side
3. Lady #2 - friend died, upset
4. Lady #3 - in hospital again
5. Lady #4 - daughter had another stroke

(11)   -   **Terrorist Attack!!** (I go home from work.) ... **911**!

November 2001:

(11)   -   Morn: *..."send Me a child...send Me a light... the children...the babies..."*

December 2001:

(11)   -   Before work*: "My love in you...I love you. I love you <u>now</u>. I will supply your needs. Your "assignments" cleanse you...Be careful... Trust Me... I <u>stay</u> here. "These are the Light" (the children?) The plan is JEHOVAH's. It's <u>HIS</u> plan. ...Pray ...pray.*

February 2002:

(17) - Our home church visits a church on North Ave. Blessed! GOD uses me for prophetic message (warning) for guest preacher and his wife.

March 2002:

(02) - My niece gets baptized!

(03) - **Dream** - Stairway at work: people walking down steps from the upper floor (some still going down steps to yet "another" basement level.) As I come down those steps to ground level, a coworker begins to taunt me and embarrass me so that I walked <u>away</u> from her and the people, towards the glass door and I <u>leave</u> the building and begin walking along a path with **"High" dirt walls** on both sides from having been dug out as a path. The path seemed somewhat curving slightly, yet with no end in sight. As I begin to walk along this path, I notice that up ahead, high up on the **left** side of the path, were 2 big elephants up on that higher ground, busy

eating leaves from trees and shrubs. I decided that although I didn't feel any real need to fear them if I continued to walk along the path under them, I chose **not** to go down that path any further, just in case they are disturbed and cause me a problem.

- Instead, I began to climb up the high wall on the **right side** of the path, digging my feet into the wall and pulling myself up until my hand reached the top and I felt very rich, green, moist grass up on the top level of land.

*Later, the HOLY SPIRIT told me, *"...To the right was right!"*

Much later, this dream revealed me **leaving my job, alone, before the other 30 or more people who accepted **early retirement/early buyout** in the summer of **2004**! (I left about a month before the rest, to not waste any summer fun with my family.) Why wait another month? I had plans!!! (See June 02, 2004.)

(06 - "...10x5 = 50 *"...speak and change...Be cleansed...Be careful... JESUS trusts you... chances... JESUS hears you..."*

April 2002:

(21) - The LORD tells me; *"I'll take you everywhere", joy, joy...struggle*

May 2002:

(18) - **JESUS Day Walk** - Patterson Park

July 2002:

(28) - Morn*: "Just trust JEHOVAH...The ones you know...Take Care ...These ones you know... trusting and cleansing... Be strong... Trust JEHOVAH... The plan is JEHOVAH's...Be strong... HE's strong in you... Be glorious... keep praying"* **Then led to read: Matthew 23**

September 2002:

(08) - **Ordained as <u>Deacon</u> today.**

(22) - Prayer in Basement: *"My Name is JEHOVAH" ...Wonderful... Be holy... Be*

holy... be strong...speak gloriously... take care of the ones you know... children, children, children... take care...you know...turn to the right... 2 smart children... change your heart."

October 2002:

(14) - We go out to **evangelize**! "Thank You, GOD!"

*We evangelize at a different location in the city...

*While evangelizing and <u>crossing the street</u>, I felt a <u>blow</u> against (inside?) my head with a "snap" light and it made me suddenly very dizzy and <u>blinded</u> me until I thought I was going to lose conscientiousness (...while I was still crossing the street!), but it <u>quickly</u> passed and I *continued* across the street. (Could the enemy of the air/territory be angry? Or is this physical?)

December 2002:

(09) - Morn. (5AM) - *"...Pray, pray, pray... Strike 3...speak... be strong... sending... Behold, it's true...Fall into My hands..."* Led to read: Judges 2:16-3:4

(25) - **<u>"HAPPY BIRTHDAY, JESUS!"</u>** Led to read: Hosea 6+7 - Obedience is better than sacrifice. GOD doesn't want sacrifices. He wants our loyalty... our trust...our lifelong service... to do what is right, love mercy, and walk humbly with Him.

<u>Year 2003 +</u>

During this 2003 year, I have had quite a few dreams and visions of ministry warnings, spiritual guidance, people warnings, scripture guidance, and spiritual encounters from my LORD.

June 2004:

Before retiring this year, I keep envisioning a **school bus** with an **Evangelism** symbol on the side of the bus. It involved a tall **candle** on top (?) of the bus. The bus was to collect the people and teach them and help them.... (I even drew a picture of it!)

-The concept had settled so deeply in my heart that after I retired, I actually went to a bus lot near me and consulted the owner as to how I may buy one of his old school buses for evangelism purposes (with my retirement "buy-out" money). He later showed me some old school buses that were being retired from service that I may want to use. My grandkids and I boarded several "very old" buses to check them out. It was fun for the kids and me, comparing buses and checking out the dashboard operations. (I hadn't the remotest idea about buses or even trying to operate one.) Still, it was fun for us.

-Then, when I inquired about the buses from friends I knew who owned a bus service company, they promptly told me about the high insurance, the need to have the bus painted, the liabilities, and that I would need the proper lot on which to park the bus. Needless to say, I was daunted by all the requirements and I gave up on the idea.

(05) - Woke up at 5:30 AM - *"Speak everywhere... Walk in the LORD... Train... I train you... Freehold in the LORD... Sing...Praise Him!...Be Ready... PRAY...cleanse...change your heart... Be Holy... I take Care of you... transfer... I love you...struggle in the LORD... Train... Plan... Credit in the LORD..."*

October 2004:

(08) - Downstairs, 6 AM: *"Take credit in JEHOVAH... Take credit in JESUS... Security... Transfer... Trust JEHOVAH... Trust JESUS... I love you... Be Ready... Rejoice...Walk right... talk right..."* Led to read: Proverbs 12

December 2004:

(05) - **DREAM:** I dream of me with JESUS! I was on my knees praying to Him right at His feet. We were both wearing white garments! Led to read: Dan. 3

(17)   -   Around 6:30 AM, after waking my niece to do her failed chores; Then we had prayer: ***"Glorify Me!.. glorify Me... Trust Me... If you love Me... glorify Me... talk right... be strong... train... if you glorify Me... take credit in the LORD... train... train all the way... 3 ways you know... if you love Me... I train you."*** Led to read: 1 Timothy 4:1-5:7.

June 02, 2004 was my last day of work/Retirement Day at my government job. (I left out at 11:30 AM and Mom & I went out to lunch.) The other 30 or so retiring people stayed at the job until the last day of June.

I worked diligently for the government for 30+ years and received many awards. GOD has also used me in the work place in so many ways that I really wouldn't know how to explain it on mere paper.

During my last year of employment I began to feel as though the hours spent on my job were "getting in the way" of quality time for the LORD. My heart kept yearning to be "out there", doing something else instead of "in here" sitting at a desk. Although my government position was extremely important and highly sensitive, it just doesn't compare with working for GOD the Creator; His benefits far outweigh man's rewards.

I began silent prayers to my LORD that if it was His Will for me, then I was certainly ready for an early out from this government job to work for Him. Well, of course, even though everyone said that it was highly unlikely that we would ever get an early out from our essential jobs any time soon, my Heavenly Father answered my prayers...<u>again</u>!

All were surprised when the opportunity was announced. <u>He just keeps on blessing me</u>!

I continue to be awed by all GOD has done and is still doing with my life; how He gave me a supernatural awakening to Who he is, then gave me a new language and **walk-on-water faith** in Him. He gave me such peace and sweet joy! The gifts and blessings GOD has bestowed upon me for His purpose keeps me mindful of how real and how powerfully <u>wonderful</u> He is.

I love Him so and I don't want anything or anyone to come before my service and my gratitude to my GOD JEHOVAH.

*GOD <u>told</u> me, "Tell them My Name; My Name is **<u>JEHOVAH</u>**."

(I want to be obedient to my LORD ... and highly favored.) When I retired in **June 2004**, I had plenty awaiting me: I had finally got custody of my five year old grandson (my oldest grandson) to live with me; In this year, I began training him and my teenage niece in Home School under a Christian, private school mentorship; They certainly were raised up in the church: learning, singing, puppetry, plays, dance ministry, gleaning, music, visiting Christian Farms ...you name it! My niece even later qualified to be accepted at a Country School ...but I couldn't afford it. In January 2006, I also took my mother into my home for 7 years. (My mom just pass on this summer.) So, we had a full and busy house! We all traveled, trained, and trusted GOD's provisions.

...Fast Forward...

GOD has taken me from church Usher to Treasurer, to Deacon, to Youth Pastor/Elder, and today, in the <u>present year of **2016**</u>, GOD has made a way and chose me to shepherd a loving group of seniors in Bible Study and in preaching the Word at a senior building on the 2nd and 4th <u>Saturdays</u>. (Shabbat!) - (*Yes, GOD can make use of an old filthy rag like me.*)

*GOD also had sent me to serve occasionally at yet another church over the past 6 or 7 years. Praise GOD.

*There are so many more blessings, testimonies, dreams, and GOD encounters in the years between all of this that I may have to do a follow-up edition:

I will tell you of my trip to Jerusalem right after retirement where the witches and demons also came on the tour and how they reacted and what they were doing to some people. I have much <u>more</u> to share.

Our GOD wants us to know Him and to know that the spiritual is as **real**, if not <u>more</u> real, than what we see in the physical. Thus, we must desire/have a personal relationship with GOD the FATHER, GOD the SON, and GOD the

HOLY SPIRIT... our ELOHIM. We must be <u>light</u> in this dark world; we must be strong in the LORD, never doubting HIM; we must be obedient to the Word of GOD and <u>do</u> what it says do and not compromise our faith for the world or anyone or anything; we must surrender daily to JEHOVAH and let the HOLY SPIRIT guide us (walk in the spirit); we must put on the whole armor of GOD *(Ephesians 6:10-13)*...we must PRAY, PRAY, PRAY! Yet, as children of GOD, with <u>authority</u> from our LORD JESUS CHRIST, we must fear <u>nothing</u> but the LORD our CREATOR, of Whom <u>all</u> things are created by Him and are subject to Him. Amen!

For the eyes of the LORD are over the righteous, and His ears are open unto their prayers: but the face of the LORD is against them that do evil. And who is he that will harm, if ye be followers of that which is good? But and if ye suffer for righteousness' sake, happy are ye: and be not afraid of their terror, neither be troubled; But sanctify the LORD GOD in your hearts; and *be ready always* to give an answer to every man that asketh you a reason of the hope that is in you with meekness and fear: ... ***1 Peter 3:12-15***

For we have not received the spirit of bondage again to fear; but ye have received the SPIRIT of adoption, whereby we cry, ABBA, Father. **Romans 8:15**

The fear of man bringeth a snare: but whoso putteth his trust in the LORD shall be safe. **Proverbs 29:25**

Be not afraid of sudden fear, neither of the desolation of the wicked, when it cometh. For the LORD shall be thy confidence, and shall keep thy foot from being taken. **Proverbs 3:25,26**

HE shall cover thee with His feathers, and under His wings shalt thou trust: His truth shall be thy sheild and buckler. Thou shalt not be afraid for the terror by night; nor the arrow that flieth by day; Nor for the pestilence that walketh in darkness; nor for the destruction that wasteth at noonday. **Psalm 91:4-6**

The LORD is my light and my salvation; whom shall I fear? the LORD is the strength of my life; of whom shall I be afraid? When the wicked, even mine enemies and my foes, came up against me to eat up my flesh, they stumbled and fell. Though an host should encamp against me, my heart shall not fear; though war should rise against me, in this will I be confident. **(Psalm 27:1 ...)**

GOD is SPIRIT, *and he that worship Him must worship Him in spirit and in truth.*

I desire to be fully equipped for GOD's service. I hope to gain strength in sound doctrine, to rightly divide GOD's Word unto clear understanding for all, and to not deviate from the Word of GOD which was divinely given to man, His chosen Jews. (Never forget that JESUS was a Jew!) I pray to know and breathe **GOD's TRUTH**. *Amen.*

Barukh attah ADONAI Eloheinu
meleckh-ha'olam. (Hebrew)
Praised be You, O LORD our GOD, King of the universe.

Shalom!

...Ye shall know the truth, and the truth shall set you free.

Printed in the United States
By Bookmasters